Pygmies of Central Africa

Less than 1.5 metres (5 feet) tall, the Pygmies have lived in Central Africa for at least 4,000 years and probably very much longer. It has been estimated that perhaps 100,000 Pygmies still survive, living by hunting and gathering food in the tropical rain forest. In recent years, however, their lives have been increasingly affected by a succession of outside influences: European rule, post-colonial wars, and the economic and social reforms brought about by the new African governments. In this book, the author, an anthropologist who has lived among the Pygmies of the Ituri Forest, describes their way of life and explains the difficulties they are facing in adjusting to a changing world.

Original Peoples

PYGMIES
OF CENTRAL AFRICA

Schuyler Jones

Wayland

Original Peoples

Eskimos — The Inuit of the Arctic
Maoris of New Zealand
Aborigines of Australia
Plains Indians of North America
South Pacific Islanders
Indians of the Andes
Indians of the Amazon
Bushmen of the Kalahari
Pygmies of Central Africa
Bedouin — The Nomads of the Desert
The Zulus of Southern Africa
Lapps — Reindeer Herders of Lapland

Frontispiece *An archer from the Mbuti group of Pygmies, who live in the Ituri Forest.*

First published in 1985 by
Wayland (Publishers) Limited
61 Western Road, Hove
East Sussex BN3 1JD, England

© Copyright 1985 Wayland (Publishers) Limited

Phototypeset by Planagraphic Typesetters Limited
Printed in Italy by G. Canale & C.S.p.A., Turin
Bound in the U.K. by The Garden City Press
Limited, Herts.

British Library Cataloguing in Publication Data

Jones, Schuyler
  Pygmies of Central Africa. — (Original peoples)
  1. Pygmies 2. Africa, Central — Description
  and travel — 1981-
  I. Title II. Series
  305.8'967   GN651

ISBN 0-85078-584-7

Contents

Introduction

The cool, green shady world of the rain forest of tropical Africa.

The Pygmies of Africa live in the equatorial rain forests that stretch from the Rwenzori Mountains, west of Lake Victoria, across into West Africa. The earliest records of their existence in this part of the world date from the Sixth Dynasty of Ancient Egypt, more than 4,000 years ago. Other early accounts come from Greek and Roman historians, who used the term 'pygmy' to describe the small people who lived beyond the boundaries of the then known world.

Today the term 'pygmy' is used to describe those hunter-gatherer peoples in Asia and Africa who are of small stature, that is, less than 1.5 metres (5 feet) tall.

This book is about those Pygmies who live in the large tropical rain forests of Central Africa. To them the forest is the real world and it provides just about everything they need or want. Until recently this was one of the most isolated areas of Africa.

The rain forest of the Congo basin is not the impenetrable, steamy jungle that is described in some books and films. It is a cool, green, shady world, protected from the tropical sun by a leafy canopy that is more than 46 metres (150 feet) above

6

the forest floor. However strange and forbidding this forest may seem to outsiders, it is an environment that provides food and shelter in abundance for people, like the Pygmies, who know and understand it.

The Pygmies are so well adapted to their forest environment that they have no need for domestic animals and do not plant crops. They live, for the most part, on what the forest has to offer. For this reason, some anthropologists have described the hunting and gathering way of life as the most persistent and successful adaptation that man has ever made to his environment.

This book tells the story of the Pygmy forest hunters, their way of life, and the difficulties they are facing in adjusting to a rapidly changing world.

A Pygmy hunter, equipped with knife, spear and net.

Chapter 1 **People of the forest**

Who are the Pygmies?

The term 'pygmy' is used to describe those human populations which average less than 1.5 metres (5 feet) in height. Such people are found in widely separated parts of the world, each group having its own social and economic organization as well as its own systems of belief. Interest in such peoples, from the earliest records down to recent times, has tended to be superficial, concentrating on the physical size of what have sometimes been called 'equatorial dwarf tribes'.

Research in the last 30 years has rightly shown that the Pygmies in Central Africa have the same sorts of complex religious beliefs, social organization, economic institutions, and ways of life, as other hunter-gatherer peoples.

Perhaps the most interesting thing about hunter-gatherer peoples is the remarkable extent to which they live in harmony with their environment. They make fewer demands on the resources of their territory than any other peoples. Their hunting territories are large; their numbers are few; and their hunting methods are such that they can never pose a threat to the survival of any species of animal. Their huts are small and easily constructed of light, flexible saplings, bark strips, and leaves; firewood is plentiful and everywhere available in the form of fallen branches. Pygmies do not plant crops, so they do not need to cut down trees. Thus they are not destroying their forest home. They are a natural part of the tropical forest.

A Pygmy man with his young son.

The term 'pygmy' is used to describe people who are less than 1.5 metres (5 feet) tall.

The forest world

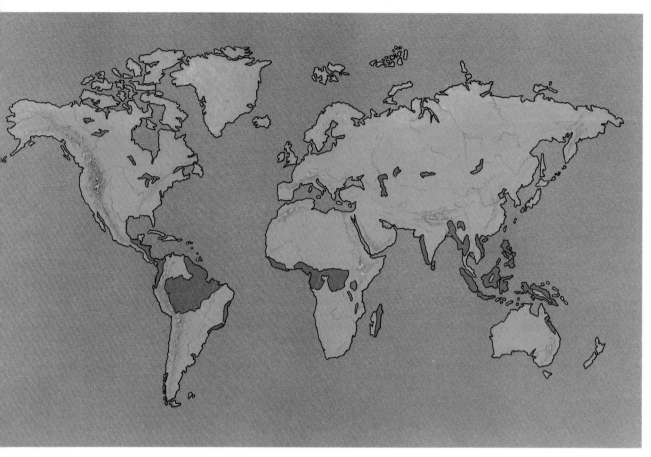

The green areas of this map show the tropical rain forests of the world.

The great rain forests of Central Africa cover an area of 175 million hectares — an area roughly ten times the size of the British Isles. Here the annual temperatures are between 20°C (68°F) and 29°C (85°F) and the rainfall is in excess of 2,030 mm (80 inches) each year. There is no marked seasonal change, no rainy or dry season; it may rain at any time of the year. Until recently, there were few roads or large towns; only the rivers served as natural highways into the interior.

The average height of the taller trees in the rain forest is 46 to 55 metres (150 to 180 feet), though individual trees over 60 metres (200 feet) are not uncommon. The variety of trees is bewildering. There are seldom less than 40 species of trees per hectare and sometimes over 100. These trees grow very straight and slender and do not branch out till

10

near the top. One characteristic of the tropical rain forest is that trees of different height form layers, 'a forest above a forest' as it has been described. The forest interior is dark, cool, and damp and there are only small patches of sunlight scattered about.

This is the home of the Pygmy and of a great variety of wild life, such as chimpanzees, gorillas, okapis, baboons, elephants, buffaloes, leopards, monkeys, dwarf hippopotamuses, tree hyraxes and, among a wealth of bird life, the rare Congo peacock. It is a hunter's paradise.

Above *Until recently, there were few roads into the forest: the rivers served as natural highways into it.* **Below** *This diagram shows the different layers of the tropical rain forest.*

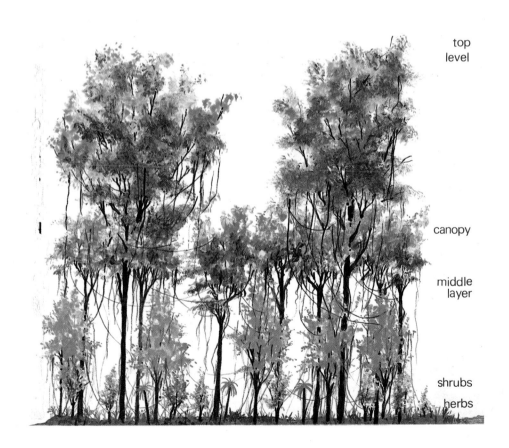

top level

canopy

middle layer

shrubs

herbs

Tribal groupings

A Mbuti camp in the heart of the Ituri Forest, in Zaire.

There are three main groups of African Pygmies living in the equatorial forest region. These are the Mbuti of the Ituri Forest, the Tswa of the western Congo and western Africa, and the Twa who live between Lake Kivu and Lake Tanganyika. Some consider only the first to be true Pygmies, as they are all less than 1.5 metres (5 feet) in height and are relatively free from intermarriage with neighbouring farming peoples. From the evidence we have, it seems that the Mbuti of the Ituri Forest, more than any of the others, still preserve their original nomadic way of life as hunters and gatherers.

The Mbuti have been subdivided into three major groups according to language: the Aka, who speak Mangbetu; the Sua, who speak Bira; and the Efe, who speak Lese. The Efe are archers, and the Sua are primarily people who hunt with nets. The size of these hunting groups varies from 3 to 37 huts among the archers, but the average group is about 6 families. Among net hunters, the average group is about 15 families. The total number of Mbuti is about 35 to 40,000, living in an area of 100,000 square kilometres (386,100 square miles).

This map shows where the main groups of Pygmies live in Central Africa.

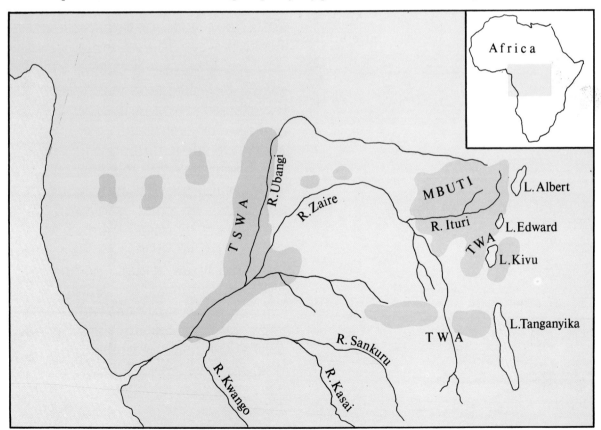

The hunter-gatherers' way of life

If we could look back 100,000 years or more, we would find that all the peoples in the world were hunters and gatherers. It was the success of this way of life over tens of thousands of years that ensured the survival of the human race. It provided the basis for everything that has since been accomplished.

Hunter-gatherer peoples are nomads. They live in small groups in hunting camps and on most days the men go hunting while the women go out to gather nuts, berries and tubers. After living in the same camp for three or four weeks, the amount of food that can be gathered in the area has been greatly reduced and the game that has not been caught by the hunters has probably been scared away. So, temporarily, the resources of the area round the camp have been reduced. The people move to another campsite and the process begins all over again.

The empty huts of an abandoned Pygmy campsite in the forest.

A Pygmy woman making a belt from natural fibres found in the forest.

However even the most favourable environment does not necessarily offer everything the people want. The Pygmies of Central Africa solved this problem by setting up trading relationships with neighbouring farming peoples. We do not know when this began or what items were originally exchanged, but it seems that the Pygmies gradually found the arrangement to be more and more useful. Not only could they get salt, tobacco, metal arrowheads and spear points in exchange for meat, but they acquired a taste for some cultivated foods, especially the plantain.

This led some observers to conclude that the Pygmies were not really self-sufficient and that they depended on trade for their survival. We now know that this is not true, for when war swept through Zaire in the years following independence, the Pygmies retreated deeper into the Ituri Forest and resumed their trade-free way of life.

15

Chapter 2 **Life with the Pygmies**

Forest camps

The Pygmies live in temporary camps in the forest, rather than permanent villages.

A typical Pygmy camp of net hunters consists of perhaps 12 to 18 round, dome-shaped huts, each about 1.5 metres (5 feet) high. The women and girls build these, first making a framework of tall thin sticks bent over and tied together at the top. Then, taking strips of bark, they lash horizontal branch stems on to this framework to strengthen it, and cover the whole structure with large green leaves. It takes about one hour to make a secure dwelling. A small fire is usually built inside, near the doorway.

During the day, if there is no hunt, the men may mend their hunting nets, make barkcloth, or gamble, using arrows instead of money. The women look after the small children,

A Pygmy mother and child outside their home in a clearing in the forest.

Young girls fetching water from a stream near their village.

cook food, collect firewood, and perhaps re-arrange the leaves on their huts to prevent the rain coming in. Young girls help their mothers by fetching water and preparing food, while the boys practise the skills they will need later as hunters.

A favourite game is to spear a moving object. A bundle of leaves the size of a football is tied to a long strip of bark and a boy swings this round so that it just skims the ground. Several boys with sharpened sticks try to spear it as it flashes past. Among Pygmies, hunting is a game, a sport, and a way of life.

Hunting in the forest

Apart from a dog or a few chickens, Pygmies do not keep any animals.

Pygmies make a living by the hunting of game and the gathering of wild forest products, which is why they are called hunter-gatherer peoples. They do not plant crops and, except for a few dogs and an occasional chicken or two, they do not keep any domestic animals. They live off what the environment has to offer.

The women do all the gathering,

putting the foods they find in their baskets, while the men hunt antelope, buffalo, and other animals, including the rare okapi. There is plenty of food waiting to be collected and the forest provides an ideal environment for many kinds of game. The Pygmies make use of these resources by cooperation, rather than competition.

Every Pygmy man carries a bow, arrows, and a spear when he goes hunting. In some parts of the Ituri Forest the men also carry nets which they have made from plant fibres. Each net is some 12 to 18 metres (40 to 60 feet) long and just over 1 metre (4 feet) wide. The women go quietly ahead through the forest, collecting edible berries and nuts as they go. The men set up their nets among the trees and undergrowth, each man attaching his net to those of his neighbours on either side. When all is ready, a signal is given and the women advance toward the nets, shouting and clapping their hands. Running to escape this noise, the animals soon begin to crash into the nets. They are quickly killed by the waiting hunters, and the meat is packed into the women's baskets.

A hunting group sets off in search of game in the forest.

Gathering

The Pygmies, although famous as hunters, actually obtain most of their food by gathering roots, vegetables, fruits, nuts, and fungi in the forest. Gathering is considered women's work, a job that includes the collection of snails, grubs, termites, ants, larvae, and, occasionally, fish and freshwater crabs. Unlike hunting, gathering is an individual rather than a group activity.

Although there is little seasonal variation in the tropical forest, certain nuts and fruits are more plentiful in January and February. The food most highly prized by Pygmies is honey. Gathering honey is considered men's work, because it involves tree climbing. The women go along to be certain of getting their share. The equipment needed for honey gathering is fire and an axe. When the honey tree has been located, one man climbs up to investigate, while the others, using glowing embers brought from camp, get a fire going. Several sticks, their glowing ends together, are then tied up in a bundle of large green leaves. This is hauled up the tree on a vine rope and used to smoke out the bees.

Then, after a few minutes' work with an axe to enlarge the hole, the Pygmy can reach in to remove the honey. Although often covered with bees during this operation, the Pygmies are either not stung, or do not mind being stung.

Some tropical-forest bees make their hives in the ground. These bees do not sting and the women gather this honey themselves. The Pygmies make containers of bark and sometimes vine baskets lined with leaves to carry honey. The discovery of honey creates a party atmosphere and everyone, especially the children, is in a happy mood.

Left *A half-finished basket, which will be used to gather food from the forest.*

A Pygmy climbing a palm tree.

Sharing food

Sharing food is a characteristic of hunter-gatherer peoples. Each animal killed on a hunt is divided up and shared out according to complex rules. It is in the best interests of everyone to cooperate in this way. In the first place, successful hunting is usually achieved by group effort. In the second place, food-sharing rules act as a kind of insurance. If a man or women cannot hunt because of illness or injury, their families receive a share anyway.

The main food-sharing rule applies to those who take part in the hunt, either directly or indirectly. Thus the owner of a dog, that was seen to chase an animal to the point where it was killed, may claim a share. If a bow and arrow or hunting net has been borrowed and an animal is killed with the arrow or becomes entangled in the net and is killed, then the owner of the bow and arrow or net is entitled to a share of it. In the same way, if an animal is killed with a borrowed spear, the owner of the spear is entitled to a share.

The rules of food-sharing are many and complex, but they all ensure that whatever is caught is fairly shared among all the members of the group.

Left *A hunter with a small animal that he has caught.*

Any animal caught on a hunt is divided up and shared between the hunters according to complex rules.

Village farmers

The tropical rain forests of Central Africa provide an ideal environment for a hunting and gathering way of life, but hunting and gathering is not the only way of making a living in these forests. Probably from a very early time, non-Pygmy peoples have made their homes in the rain forest. They have used the environment in a very different way from the Pygmies. In order to plant crops, they have made large clearings in the forest and have built permanent villages. The main crops they raise are plantains, manioc, peanuts, maize, rice and beans.

These farming people do not feel at home in the forest; they prefer their hot, sunny clearings. They are poor hunters and rarely venture far into the surrounding forests for any

These two women from a non-Pygmy tribe are planting maize in a forest clearing.

Trading relationships have developed between Pygmy groups and people in villages, like this one, which are outside the forest.

reason. Because they do not hunt and because they cut down trees, the Pygmies have little respect for these villagers. But the village farmers grow crops, especially plantains, that the Pygmies want, and they have blacksmiths who make axes, metal arrowheads, knife blades, and spear points that the Pygmies find useful. They can also provide salt, tobacco, and other luxuries that the Pygmies like.

Plantains, which are a variety of large cooking banana, are the only food that the Pygmies regularly eat which is not found growing wild in the forest. Plantains differ from ordinary bananas in that when ripe they are starchy rather than sweet.

So the Pygmies and the villagers engage in trade and both parties benefit from the relationship. Gradually the contact between these two very different cultures has grown to include not only trade, but certain magical practices, dances and festivities, and ceremonies connected with birth, marriage and death.

25

Chapter 3 **European explorers**

Origin and history

As far as we know, Pygmies from earliest times inhabited the Ituri Forest region and from there they gradually spread over the whole of equatorial Africa. Until recently, no archaeological excavations had ever been attempted in the tropical forests of Africa. At the time of writing, the few excavations that have been carried out have not thrown any light on the history and origin of the Pygmies.

Stone tools, particularly stone axes, are sometimes found in the forests, but the Pygmies do not

Below and opposite *These pictures were taken at the turn of the century by a photographer on an expedition that went in search of Pygmies.*

recognize them or understand their use. Like peoples in other parts of the world, they associate them with lightning. The earliest known accounts of the Pygmies do not link their technology with the use of stone tools, though they may have made and used them in the past.

Whatever their origin and history, both the Pygmies and the farming villagers agree that the Pygmies are the original inhabitants of the tropical forest.

Exploration

David Livingstone's boat being swamped by an irate hippopotamus.

Although several ancient accounts from Greece and Egypt mention the Pygmies of Central Africa, from the sixth century AD to the nineteenth century — 1,300 years — nothing more was heard of them. It was assumed that the earlier reports were based on myth. Then, in the years between 1860 and 1870, the Pygmies were re-discovered as European explorers began to unravel more and more of the mysteries of Africa's interior. This period of exploration was motivated by several unsolved

28

problems. Foremost among these was locating the source of the Nile. Solving this problem had been the dream of geographers and explorers for generations. It was in pursuit of this goal that the great rain forests of the Congo basin were explored.

In the nineteenth century, David Livingstone explored the upper Congo River, following its course as it flowed northwards for over 1,600 km (1,000 miles). But he did not know it was the Congo, nor did anyone else at the time. Since it flowed north, it might be the Nile. Livingstone died in 1873 with this question unanswered. Then in 1876 the Welsh explorer, Henry Stanley, decided to follow the river on from the point where Livingstone had stopped. By July 1877 Stanley had traced its course for more than 2,575 km (1,600 miles) and proved that it was the Congo River.

In the decade that followed, Henry Stanley crossed and re-crossed much of the Congo basin and encountered the Pygmies on numerous occasions. In his writings he expressed the misconceptions and prejudices of his day, describing them as living 'the life of human beasts in morass and fen and jungle wild'. One Englishman, James Harrison, took six Pygmies to London in 1905. Dressed in Victorian fashion, they remained his guests for two years before he returned them to Africa. To his critics he replied, 'think of how much good it may do when these . . . people return, and round the campfires tell over and over again the wonders and kindness of the white masters'. What the Pygmies thought of it all has not been recorded.

Henry Stanley met many Pygmy groups during his exploration of the Congo basin.

29

Language

Discussing the day's events.

Language is one aspect of culture that often enables scientists to understand something of the history and origin of a people where there are no written records. Unfortunately that does not help in this case. Most Pygmies speak two or three different languages — a necessity in their frequent dealings with various neighbouring peoples.

Scientists studying the Pygmies of the Ituri Forest have assumed that they once had their own language, but few, if any traces of it remain. All Ituri Pygmies speak the language or languages of the agricultural villagers with whom they maintain trading relationships. They do, however, speak these languages in their own way, with characteristic pauses and a distinctive singsong manner. What language or languages they spoke in earlier generations will probably never be known.

The clay pots (left and centre) were obtained by trade with villagers.

Chapter 4 **Social and cultural life**

Social life

Socially and economically the most important group in Pygmy society is made up of families who hunt together. The size of the group varies according to which hunting techniques are used. For those Pygmies who hunt with nets, the ideal group size is about 15 families. That is, a group which can provide 15 married men with nets. If the group falls below 10 families, hunting becomes difficult. There are not enough nets to ensure success and not enough women and children to act effectively as beaters. If the group is too large, consisting perhaps of between 20 and 30 families, it also cannot function as an efficient hunting unit, and the group splits up.

Those Pygmies who hunt with bows and arrows rather than nets live in smaller groups. This is a direct result of their different hunting techniques, which require only a few men and do not involve the women at all. Among these archers, five or six men may go hunting with their dogs, hoping to shoot animals that the dogs have put to flight. Also, one man alone may lie in wait, imitate the call of the game, and hope that an animal will approach close enough to be shot with an arrow.

There are no chiefs, headmen, or other leaders among the Pygmies. The status of an individual male depends mainly on his reputation as a hunter. An older man, highly regarded as a hunter and with a reputation for modesty and wisdom, will have some influence in camp affairs, but he cannot acquire authority

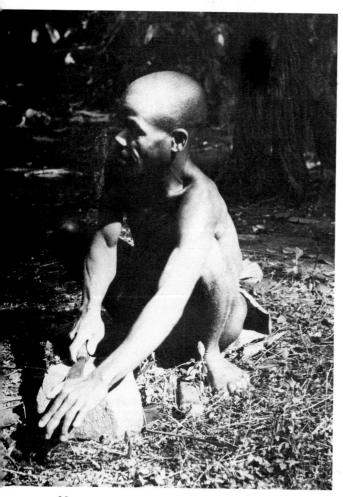

Left *A hunter sharpening a knife, obtained through trade, on a stone.*

32

There are no chiefs in a camp. A man's status depends on his skill as a hunter.

because it is not an aspect of life which the Pygmies recognize.

Decisions are reached by discussion, often round campfires at night. The men gather round a central fire in the forest camp most evenings to discuss hunting plans and any other matters requiring a group decision. Sometimes there are arguments and the talks may continue until late, but by the time everyone goes to bed, tomorrow's plans have been settled.

Marriage and family

A Pygmy man has only one wife. Together with their children, they live in their own hut, which the wife builds anew in each camp. The family thus keeps its individuality and maintains some privacy, while at the same time remaining part of the larger and more important group, the hunting band. The area round each hut is regarded as private. All food is prepared and cooked over the fire in front of the hut's entrance.

Young girls are attracted to a man

Although part of a larger group, each family has its own privacy and independence.

Pygmy children playing in their own mini-hut built by their parents.

who displays courage, skill in the hunt, and ability in dancing. There is no formal engagement ceremony. A young man gives the girl of his choice small presents and, if these are accepted, it is a sign that she agrees to the marriage proposal. The only rule that is normally observed is that the girl must come from a different hunting camp than the man.

Once she has accepted him, the girl goes with the man to his camp. There she lives with his mother, learning the rules of the camp. Sometime later, members of the girl's hunting camp pay a visit to ask for a gift of arrows, axes, and other implements, or they may ask for a bride for a man of their own hunting group. There is no marriage ceremony other than a feast and a dance to celebrate the event. The girl builds a hut and the two live together.

35

Music and art

Pygmies greatly enjoy music and dancing. The main musical instruments they use are drums and the *sanza,* neither of which they make themselves. The *sanza,* which is found over a wide area of Central Africa, is a small wooden box fitted with strips of metal. The box is held in the hands and the metal strips are played with the thumbs, making a pleasant tinkling melody. This, and the rhythmic pounding of barkcloth, is a characteristic sound in a Pygmy forest camp.

Dancing and singing round a central camp fire at night is a popular pastime. Some of the dances recreate

hunting events. In these, men and women dance separately. In addition to drums, the rhythmic beating of sticks is used as an accompaniment to the dance. Pygmies sing about hunting, about religious beliefs, and about collecting honey. They are also adept at mime and drama and frequently enact the events of the day. They like to mimic and make fun of the farming villagers nearby, but much of their singing and dancing concerns their relationships with each other, with the forest, and with all the creatures of their forest world. Thus, much of their singing is of a religious nature.

Pygmies almost never carve wood to make those types of objects which we think of as 'African art'. The few examples known are all imitations of things made by their farming neighbours. Decorative art among the Pygmies is confined to designs painted on their bodies and on barkcloth. Using a leaf stem as a brush, they apply a black dye, made from the seed pod of a gardenia, on their faces and legs. They use the same dye to paint designs on barkcloth, creating elaborate geometrical patterns.

Left *Pygmies enjoy music and dancing, often re-enacting hunting events.*

Right *The drum is one of the main musical instruments used by the Pygmies. Most of the drums owned by the Pygmies are obtained by trade and not made by themselves.*

Magic and religion

If the hunting has not been successful for several days, Pygmies may seek to improve things by singing certain songs. Magical practices are also carried out to alter weather that may adversely affect hunting. Special medicines in the form of paste made from animal parts may be rubbed on the forehead of a hunter to improve his skills. It is believed by some that additional strength and power can be obtained by the use of wooden bells hung on the body. Certain magic whistles may be used to deflect a storm or attract game.

The Pygmies believe in an all-powerful lord of the forest who rules over all life, all animals, and all people. Everything belongs to him because he created everything. He is the source of all good, all misfortune, and all death. He is offended

If offended, the lord of the forest sends leopards to a camp as a punishment.

by quarrels among people, by disrespect for elders, by the failure to make him offerings from a hunt, and other broken rules. By way of punishment, he sends leopards to the camp, causes trees to fall, and brings death, the symbol of which is the rainbow. Lightning is one of his powerful weapons. It is these abnormal conditions of the physical world that indicate his presence. At such times the hunters are careful not to be seen or attract his attention by unseemly behaviour. Storms bring what the Pygmies dislike most: water, thunder, lightning and rainbows — all of which are associated with death.

Chapter 5 **A changing way of life**

Technology

The resources of the tropical rain forest are so abundant that a few simple tools, techniques and weapons are all that are needed for Pygmies to make a living. Many of the raw materials used by other hunter-gatherers, such as animal skins, bones, clay, and stone, are scarcely used by the Pygmies. They do not work metal and rely on trade to obtain the metal artefacts which they want.

All Pygmies use fire for cooking and driving away the damp chill of night, but some, such as the Mbuti of the Ituri Forest, have no knowledge of making fire; a new fire is always lit by taking an ember from an old one. When they move from one campsite to another, they carry fire with them.

Campfires provide most of the light needed at night, but some Pygmies collect the resin from certain trees to make small torches. The resin is rolled, wrapped in leaves, and tied with strips of bark. When lit, it burns with a bright light.

Every adult male Pygmy carries a bow and a fistful of arrows whenever he goes into the forest. Some arrows have metal points and leaf flights instead of feathers. These are highly prized but seldom used for fear of losing them. Other arrows used are plain hardwood shafts, and it is these which are poisoned and used to hunt birds and monkeys. Metal tipped arrows are used mostly for hunting

Left *This metal fishing spear has been obtained by trade*

antelope. Larger game animals such as wild boar and elephant are speared.

Many of the artefacts found in hunting camps are not made by Pygmies, but by neighbouring farmers with whom they trade. Many of these items, such as musical instruments, pots and pans, carved wooden stools, and certain types of baskets, have been borrowed or stolen by Pygmies when visiting villages.

Poison being put on to the tips of arrows, prior to going out hunting in the forest.

Change

The last 30 years have brought many changes to the equatorial forest regions of Central Africa. The countries that were once colonies of various European nations are now independent. When this happened, the Pygmies had only a vague idea of what a nation was, and knew nothing about government in a national sense. In the former Belgian Congo, now Zaire, the African government decided that the Pygmies should leave the forest, abandon their hunting and gathering way of life, and take up farming or some other more productive occupation in order to make a useful contribution to the needs of a new nation.

Change itself is not new. All societies are changing and they have always been changing. What is new is the rate at which changes take place and the ability of a people such as the Pygmies to come to terms with these new changes, so different from anything they have experienced.

Following the arrival of European explorers in the nineteenth century,

Today, the rain forests of Africa are being opened up by more and more roads, like this one.

roads were gradually cut through the forests. Later bridges were built and colonial administrators and other civil servants began to appear. These were followed by anthropologists, tourists, independence, and warfare.

During the 90 years that elapsed between the arrival of the first European explorer and the departure of the last European colonial, the Pygmies were relatively unaffected by the great changes that were taking

Rapidly expanding towns and cities are part of the changing face of tropical Africa.

place in Africa. This is because, for the most part, they lived in remote isolated stretches of forest. Today, however, more and more roads are being built and the forests that have sheltered the Pygmies since ancient times are being cut down.

The future

Will these two Pygmy women soon be giving up forest life for village life?

The forest world in which the Pygmies have lived for thousands of years is vanishing. It is estimated that the tropical forests of Africa are disappearing today at the rate of more than 4,500 square miles each year. This means that the environment within which the Pygmies can continue to maintain their traditional way of life is rapidly getting smaller and smaller.

For many decades most Pygmies have developed ever closer relations with neighbouring farming peoples.

Trade has brought these very different peoples more closely together. Because the arrangement has been so useful, some Pygmies have set up camp on the edge of farming villages and now spend more time working as farm labourers and servants than before. Those left behind in the forest are spending more time hunting for meat which they can sell to villagers.

The climate of the tropical forest seems to be changing, too — or are we only just beginning to understand

44

it? It now rains less frequently in some areas than previously. Along the forest roads new towns have sprung up, filled mostly with strangers. Many Pygmies have begun to spend more and more time in settlements. Some have started to attend school and the teachers have found them to be able pupils. Some traditional Pygmy forest territories are now national parks where hunting is forbidden.

The Pygmies are gradually becoming more dependent on the village way of life and are beginning to adopt village values. Culturally, the Pygmies are changing along with a changing world.

The tropical rain forest is increasingly becoming part of Africa's disappearing world.

Glossary

Anthropologist A scientist who studies man; either ancient man or modern human societies.

Archaeological excavations The careful digging up of places by scientists to find traces of early man or past cultures.

Archaeology The scientific study of antiquities or prehistoric remains.

Archers People who are skilled in the use of bows and arrows.

Artefacts Anything made by people: tools, weapons, cloth, utensils, musical instruments, etc.

Barkcloth A kind of cloth made from bark by people who do not know the art of weaving.

Beaters People who act to scare birds or animals towards hunters so that they may be caught or shot.

Culture Learned behaviour: any skills learned by people as members of a society, including languages, technology, beliefs, music, etc.

Domestic animals Any tame animals, such as farm animals.

Fungi Certain types of plants, of which mushrooms and toadstools are the most common.

Game Animals and birds hunted for their meat.

Hyrax The tree hyrax is the only hoofed animal in the world that lives in trees.

Manioc A tropical plant with starchy roots, widely grown for food. In South America, it is known as cassava.

Mime Copying the speech, gestures, and manners of a person or animal.

Misconception An incorrect idea.

Nomad A member of a group who have no fixed home and who regularly move from place to place.

Okapi A pony-sized animal related to giraffes. It is found in only two areas in Africa.

Plantain A large starchy cooking banana.

Prejudice An unfair opinion or feeling about someone or something.

Rain forest A tropical forest receiving annual rainfall in excess of 2,030 mm (80 inches) and having temperatures between 20° to 29°C (68° to 85°F).

Resin A sticky substance obtained from the bark of trees.

Sanza A small, wooden box-shaped musical instrument producing sound from metal strips mounted on the top.

Self-sufficient A person or people who make all the things they need and grow or hunt and collect all the food they require.

Status A person's social position, rank, or standing in society.

Tuber The root of a plant.

Books to read

No other books have been written for children about the Pygmies of Central Africa. The titles listed below have been written for adults and so children may find them difficult to read. It may also be difficult to obtain the older titles which will probably only be held by large reference libraries. Further information on the lives of African Pygmies can be obtained from consulting books on jungles and on the equatorial countries of Africa, and also from encyclopedias.

Harrison, J. J. *Life Among the Pygmies of the Ituri Forest, Congo Free State* (Hutchinson, 1905)

Shebesta, P. *Among Congo Pygmies* (Hutchinson, 1933)

Shebesta, P. *Revisiting my Pygmy Hosts* (Hutchinson, 1936)

Turnbull, C. M. *The Forest People* (Chatto & Windus, 1961)

Turnbull, C. M. *Wayward Servants* (Natural History Press, New York 1965)

Turnbull, C. M. *The Mbuti Pygmies: Change and Adaptation* (Holt, Rinehart & Winston, 1983)

Picture acknowledgements

The author and the publishers would like to thank the following for allowing their pictures to be reproduced in this book: Camerapix Hutchison Library *cover,* 11 (top/Melanie Friend), 12 (Adrian Clark), 15 (Adrian Clark), 17, 24, 25, 33, 34, 42 (Sarah Errington); Bruce Coleman Limited 6 (M. P. L. Fogden), 39 (Peter Davey), 37 (WWF/Paul S. Wachtel), 43 (Christian Zuber), 45 (Christian Zuber); Mary Evans Picture Library 29; Ian Griffiths 8, 14, 18, 20; Susan Griggs 16, 19, 21, 36, 37; Schuyler Jones 7, 22, 30, 31, 32; The Mansell Collection 28; Rex Features 41; Royal Geographical Society 26, 27 (both); Vision International 35 and 44 (both by Exp. Philippart de Foy); ZEFA *frontispiece,* 9, 23. The diagrams on pages 10 and 11 are from the Wayland Picture Library. The illustrations on pages 13 and 39 were drawn by Malcolm S. Walker.

Index